AF305067

STEPMOTHER

ALSO BY HELEN MORT

Division Street
No Map Could Show Them
Black Car Burning
A Line Above the Sky
The Illustrated Woman

STEPMOTHER

Helen Mort

Chatto & Windus
LONDON

1 3 5 7 9 10 8 6 4 2

Chatto & Windus, an imprint of Vintage, is part of the
Penguin Random House group of companies

Vintage, Penguin Random House UK, One Embassy Gardens,
8 Viaduct Gardens, London SW11 7BW

penguin.co.uk/vintage
global.penguinrandomhouse.com

First published by Chatto & Windus in 2026

Set in 11/14pt Minion Pro
Typeset by Six Red Marbles UK, Thetford, Norfolk

Printed and bound in Great Britain by Clays Ltd, Elcograf S.p.A.

The authorised representative in the EEA is Penguin Random House Ireland,
Morrison Chambers, 32 Nassau Street, Dublin D02 YH68

A CIP catalogue record for this book is available from the British Library

ISBN 9781784746445

Penguin Random House is committed to a sustainable future
for our business, our readers and our planet. This book is made
from Forest Stewardship Council® certified paper.

For B & L

Contents

i.

The Armenian variant of the enigmatic 'Once upon a time' of the English and French fairytale is both utterly precise and absolutely mysterious: 'There was a time and no time.'

– Angela Carter

*Step – Old English steop-, with connotations of 'loss,' in combinations like steopcild 'orphan,' related to astiepan, bestiepan 'to bereave, to deprive of parents or children,' from Proto-Germanic *steupa- 'bereft', literally 'pushed out,' from PIE *steup-, from root *(s)teu- (1) 'to push, stick, knock,' with derivatives referring to fragments.*

i.

There was a time and no time.
Time and no word
for what was left of it

and what was left of it
got wasted. So soon! So
we helped it home

or it crawled on three legs,
lame dog, howling
at the salt-rim of the moon.

I had time and you took
too much of it. Or we had our time
and I made too much of it.

There was a time to leave
and we missed it,
so time left us instead,

air-kissed us, sent us
to bed without supper.
There should have been enough

for both of you, Time said
and there was, certainly,
but we'd already spent it –

Time would have to
deal with us later.
There is always time on paper

but in practice we have just
a handful of half-decent tales
that only time will tell

which is perhaps
our small idea of hell:
everything in due course,

the pause we're living in
before the end of time
and how we try to stop it

despite ourselves,
line after line
after line.

On silence

Smile, says the photographer and you bare your teeth.

You are on the terrace of a Greek hotel at dusk. The heat of the day has sunk and settled on your skin. You can smell suncream and fried fish, hear plates colliding in the kitchen. Below, the harbour's minty cool. The photographer takes your arm, steers the three of you together: tanned man, visibly pregnant woman, teenager in a white dress. You put your hand to your stomach and feel your son shift.

A flash freezes you there, awkward trio, leaning together like plants.

The photographer has a wolfish face. He wipes beads of sweat from his forehead, checks the exposure, then he gestures to you and B.

Girls only now. A photo with Mum.

One day, the picture will sit in your son's nursery, cradled in a cheap white frame. In the background you can pick out boats made tiny by sky. B.'s fair hair is bleached by Lindos sun. Her face is open. Yours is hardened by a silence you didn't know how to break. You wanted to say then: *she's not my daughter. She already has a mum.* To speak would have seemed like a disavowal, a distancing. To stay silent meant taking something which was not yours.

So of course you said nothing. You took it.

In every house there is a cupboard like this. It is usually on the top floor, facing a window which admits the night. The carpet is scrappier here, liver-coloured, and there is fat dust in the corners. The doors are made of a cheerful, inviting kind of wood. Behind them, an avalanche waits. Duvets and pillow slips. A dismantled cot, the pupae of sleeping bags, a length of green rope. Unspooling the contents, you can't help but move performatively. You are a cheap magician, pulling long scarves from a hat. Another bedsheet. A bag-within-a-bag. When you lean into the cupboard, you could pitch yourself right down the house's throat.

On origins (i)

'Better a serpent than a stepmother', Euripides said. For a moment, you like the idea of being a single line, winding around everything you touch. A vine. You have a snake tattooed on your left thigh and hip, its tongue forking onto your stomach, tasting the air. It hurt like hell, your skin bruised yellow afterwards but you like that kind of pain, because it is the kind you have chosen, the kind you can control.

/

Bruno Bettelheim: 'the typical fairy-tale splitting of the mother into a good (usually dead) mother and an evil stepmother serves the child well – the fantasy of the wicked stepmother not only preserves the good mother intact, it also prevents having to feel guilty about one's angry wishes about her'. He makes it seem as if they are twins, or one body which divides, the two halves always trying to find each other.

You only come here at night, when your toddler is sighing in his bed, when your husband and his two teenagers are sleeping or mesmerised by screen-light. This is when the urge to impose order comes, to itemise the contents of hidden places, remind yourself what is important and what might be lost. There in the left-hand corner: a solid trunk with a rusty clasp. You drag it forwards, straining your back. *Like lifting a corpse* you think though you've never done that. There is a padlock hanging open and in seconds you are lifting the lid. You stare down into a well, dark and bottomless. Without thinking, you shout. The house groans back at you. *Hello, hello, hello.* You push your forearm in, obscenely far and grope around. A shoe, a ruby sandal with a slightly arrowed toe, the heel a weapon. The sole is wet with blood. Slimy. Snake-like. You drop it. You slam the case shut and bundle coats on top of it and sit braced against the cupboard door, waiting to breathe again.

All names have been changed

Stepmothers, further than the eye can see! Stepmother disguised
as ancient yew tree. Stepmother marching towards Dunsinane
or Stepmother as house-with-no-name, as fault, as dubious
insurance claim. Stepmother as original Walk of Shame.

Stepmother as bad actor, or stepmother as dish-washer,
place-setter, place-taker, risk factor. Stepmother as mirror
facing mirror on an otherwise plain wall, muttering
who is the fairest fairest fairest of them all? Stepmother

as invisibility cloak, as cog, as hoist, as bicycle spoke.
Stepmothers all vanishing in unison, one lavish puff of smoke
and gone. Stepmother – not broke, but can't fix it.
Stepmother as taking the last biscuit. Stepmother as precipice,

Grand Canyon, as abyss. Stepmother as mis-timed lunge
for mis-planned kiss. Stepmother as mother climbing
to the highest step and waving to the family, *oh hi, hello down there!*
Then Stepmother as jump, as gathering speed, breakneck.

The next evening you go back. You manage to lean your weight against the trunk and upend it. Nothing happens at first. A sound like water retreating down a plug hole, a gurgling, rushing noise. Then there is a dark ribbon coming out, a moving, living thing, punctuated with dots of light. You think *river.* Then you think *night sky.* There must be hundreds of them, some single and some neatly paired, their laces tied together. Battered leather sandals. Comfortable brogues. A vintage Doc Marten with yellow-flecked laces and the sole coming away. There are kitten heels with a snakeskin effect and brick-like platforms. Cute hi tops. You realise you are standing with your back to the wall, retreating. They keep bumping onto the floor. A satin ballet shoe with a darned toe slips past you and tumbles down the stairs. Your first thought is that they must belong to The Ex. But when you look at them, when you lift the tongues up, they are all different sizes. And besides, you've seen her tasteful boots, how they match her 70s sheepskin jackets. You pick two at random, an almost child-sized loafer and one of the towering patent shoes. You don't need to try them on to know it: every single one of these impossible fucking shoes fits.

On origins (ii)

Not *about*. Not *with*. The condition of the stepmother is *on*. To be put on, placed. Upon-a-time. Or perhaps to be forced onto, to be grafted, to be put on top of something and left there.

If the life you've chosen is an ascent, a kind of grand ballroom staircase that leads towards your future happiness, what is the surface made of? Who steps on who?

Imagine the family, vaulting over one another. One endless game of leapfrog where you swap positions, covering the distance of the playing field with remarkable speed. Summer and mild hayfever. The squash in plastic cups on the fold-out table. The remnants of new mown grass and the indents on everyone's knees. Daisy chains. A buttercup held under the chin in playful interrogation.

/

In John Gamble's *An Irish Wake* (1826) he writes of a woman soon to die, who instructs her successor to 'be kind to my children'. As Gamble puts it, after her death the injunction was quickly forgotten and that the new woman 'proved a very step-mother'.

You think of the donkey stones that women used to polish, keeping up appearances. A step towards motherhood? Or a step that you trip over as you try to climb your way upstairs? A steep mother, like a mountain that cannot be climbed, cannot even be penetrated or seen through its death-shroud of mist.

Slipper

What if the sisters weren't ugly,
& the stepmother only usually cruel?
What if they all walked home together
after school, sharing fuchsia bubblegum?

What if ashes festered in the grate
and nobody rose to light the fire
in that low-ceilinged house
of women. What if they each desired

the other? And if the pumpkin remained vegetable
the mice carried on their secret lives
and midnight passed without incident
and moonlight was a long knife

that pared the palace garden, where the Prince
walked, cradling a glass stiletto
bought only for himself, what if his want
was a high shelf he'd built and decorated,

lined with wigs and stick-on jewels?
What if he stopped beside the ornamental pond
with its monstrous koi and – face held in the water –
tried the damn shoe on?

On origins (iii)

Hippolytus, 428 BCE: The stepmother commits suicide to prevent herself from following through on her lust for her stepson and leaves a note falsely claiming that the stepson had raped her.

You see The Ex's immortalised, frozen face and cropped blonde hair about twice a month when your stepdaughter gets the urge to uncover old albums on the iPad, piecing together her babydom and toddlerhood. Your partner has kept so much. Photos of the kids, yes, videos of them having baths and skidding down snow slopes on poly bags and crafting elaborate battles with plastic knights, but also pictures of her – the woman who you see often in real life, the woman who has a name beyond Ex, who you often feel sympathy with, often admire, even. There is something about these static images that ignites a helpless rage. Your jealousy so flammable. Here is your husband fifteen years ago, in hospital scrubs, handsome and dishevelled, anticipating his daughter's birth. Here are holiday pictures from Turkey and Morocco, children carried on shoulders. Here are cheekbones and pursed, rose petal lips. Sometimes it is worse when you know that she was behind the camera: the intensity in your husband's stare was for her. They are mementos from a past you cannot fully imagine, tangible reminders that you are only here because she decided to end things, that you are someone he might never have loved if she hadn't stopped loving him.

Step –

The greatest gift, given
without permission –

the opportunity to love
her children

On souls

In Duncan Williamson's 'The Traveller Cinderella and the Turkey Girl', the role of the wicked stepmother is played by the unjust political system. Some Cinderella stories involve fathers desiring or even raping their biological daughters. We don't talk about that. We remember the stepmother, her open mouth, her laughter.

/

As a child, you used to confuse *sole* with *soul*. You would write: *the soul of the shoe was worn with the miles it had travelled*. But sole is an infinitely better word. It also means solitary, single purpose. It means turning to the direction you want to go in and facing it down, deciding there is nothing else to do but walk. It means you are the only one who can do this.

Wicked queen

The grand ballroom, tide of white roses
        and 'At Last' by Etta James,
                treacle, sticky. They cleave together,

Woman & Prince, her dark hair
        resting on his shoulder. Hips close,
                guests cava-flushed,

cheering. A bridesmaid puts
        a rose between her teeth
                waltzes with herself, bright meringue

and when the lights go out on Etta's final note
                the room returns to view
                        in spotlit green,

a pair of burning shoes in the centre, a violin
        heard, somewhere out of sight,
                and then the hooded stepmother

                                led out by men

her proud back as she steps into the clogs
        and her feet sizzle, water dropped on a skillet.
                O we mustn't look away

                                as she begins to dance.

Afterwards, the
ballroom empty,
the shoes still
glowing
like coals.

Where did it slither to? At night, lying on your back, you become preoccupied with the dark, sinewy thing that preceded the torrent of shoes. Even now, it could be lurking in your son's bedroom, behind the blackout curtains, or hiding in the bathroom, furled behind the plants you are so bad at caring for. What if it crawls into your open mouth when you're asleep and stops your throat, or goes deeper, winds around your heart and squeezes? You scroll through the worst news, the worst-case studies. November 2021. Arthur Labinjo-Hughes, alone in a hallway for 14 hours a day. Made to drink salt water, pushed against walls by his stepmother Emma. The bruises blamed on rough play. Malnourished. What if it goes deeper, winds around your heart and squeezes? Gaunt. Found dead. 130 injuries logged. Falling through the gaps in the net, missed by social services. You think about your own son, under his leopard-spot blanket, holding his stuffed panda in one hand and his beloved 'Lancelot' wooden sword in the other. You wonder how many times a day you draw him close just to sniff his hair, bury yourself in his musky scent. You imagine your stepson and stepdaughter as toddlers, the same large eyes and serious faces, their sturdy, fragile bodies.

East of the sun, west of the moon

A young girl born into poverty
is sold by her parents to a white bear
who wants to marry her. They share a bed

though the girl is never allowed to see him
as they sleep together. He always
leaves before daybreak. One evening,

after his breathing has settled, she lights candles,
sees his true form in their light: a handsome prince,
long hair liquid on the pillow. She kisses him

hungrily. Three drops of tallow drip from the candle
and onto his naked chest. Seeing him,
waking him, she starts a prophecy –

cursed by his wicked stepmother into bear, he's doomed
to go back to her castle, east of the sun,
west of the moon – and marry her daughter.

She looks for him in mountains, imagines tunnelling inside.
She asks the wind for directions. The North Wind
lifts her like a handkerchief and carries her like a corpse.

When she finds him, they fuck for hours, him
with his shirt on, her in her skirts, grubby
from the long journey. She sits astride him,

moves like the current of the wind that brought her to the castle.
Afterwards they hatch a plot, etcetera,
to break the spell, to make the stepmother explode.

Of course it works, of course he's freed from his bear form.
Of course sometimes the girl buries her head against his neck
and misses the tang of fur, the aftermath of blood.

On anger

Is it anger you feel? Or are your snake-scales tiny mirrors for an anger the world directs at you?

/

Stepmonster. To call something or someone monstrous is a distancing, an abdication of responsibility. By calling things 'unthinkable', we mean we are not prepared to think. Close the cupboard. Bolt the door. Push a chair against it and run.

/

Once upon a time. Twice upon a time. Thrice upon a time. You make the same mistakes over and over. You fail to meet your own standards, day after weary day. You are passive-aggressive about the collection of mould-trimmed plates and dishes in L.'s room. You resent it when he leaves the table after a meal without clearing anything up. You are too tired to go swimming after school with B. in the reservoir outside town where the water is claggy and silty and the ducks sail past giving curious looks. She cries, because she wanted it to be the best day ever. You cook their favourite foods and then become aggrieved if they don't eat them. You are preoccupied with unimportant work. You kick at the cigarette butts patterning the garden path and call them dirty. You don't keep your voice down when you should. There is too much washing in the laundry basket. There are too many teenage girls playing hide and seek in the house. You spend too long straightening your hair in front of the mirror when you should be downstairs, watching a family film. But your makeup is done. Your smile is fairytale. Tomorrow is a new day. Once upon a time. Twice upon a time.

/

Some evenings when you're clearing the pots, or up to your elbows in lukewarm water, you get a writhing feeling at your core. You think of Medusa and her lithe hair, her transformation, how her serpents turned men to stone. How she was punished for what hurt her.

You would like a pair of snake-shoes. Emerald and teal, the tail of a mermaid, a siren moaning from the rocks. Not real snake, nothing so other, so prehistoric should have to die to serve your vanity. The real so seldom looks like your imagining of things: too subtle, too believable. These would cling to your calves. Start in a v under your kneecaps and cloak your whole leg. At the toe, taper to a point. Then – the final flourish – scarlet of a little protruding tongue, curled up to meet the air.

Housesitting

You came for the black and white beagador
and the glossy spaniel, dead behind the eyes,
but grew to love the garden, tilted
with its piles of rheumy apples. Inside,
few mirrors, tall rooms without photographs,
doors bearing the names of his children.

With the house empty, you only looked
at his unmade bed. You slept on the leather
brown Chesterfield and if you pictured yourself
here it was outside with basil-mint
and the ingenuity of ivy, a sparrowhawk
menacing the bird table. You walked

through long, wet grass, admiring
his resolve to let such wild things
be, pondweed and greengages, how
the henbit and purple deadnettle
came through the gaps, and shook
their false confetti everywhere.

When did you become a stepmother? Was it the first time your stepdaughter looped her arm into yours or the first time your stepson asked you for a lift? First argument or first hug? What doorway did you step through and why is the frame no longer visible, why has it melted back into the plasterboard, sealed itself tight? Why do you have to slither through your own life to find it?

On meeting

A youth theatre production of *Chicago* – B. was in the chorus, all heavy black eye make-up and fishnets. You were in the foyer with L. He was eighteen and cat-like, six foot two and broad-shouldered, gold hoops in his ears. A tall girl and her father walked over and clapped L. on the back. *Good to see you again mate, so good to see you.* He grinned and swept his mane of hair out of his eyes. Next door below the stage, the band were tuning up, squeaks and the thrum of strings. He barely hesitated when he introduced you. *This is my stepmum.* The glow lasted well past the encore and when you walked out past Crucible corner you were a kite.

/

You first met L. at a John Grant gig with his Mum, a studio close to the University. You recognised her from parties, squinted through the blue and violet lights of the Octagon, raised a hand in greeting. *This is my son,* she said. She was not yet The Ex. She was someone you saw around town, in the arthouse cinema and the pub. On stage, John Grant's voice was a cool glass pressed against a warm cheek. The venue was circular. The spotlight haloed him, bent over the black piano, his entire body pulsing with notes. The air smelled coconut-y from the smoke machines.

/

You were standing in the living room at their Dad's house. There was a Chesterfield sofa behind you but you were unsure if you should sit down. There was a turtle's head sticking from one wall, grey-green and leathery, and a death mask above the fireplace with its eyes serenely closed. The walls were painted a rich, loam-y brown. You smiled at B. and L., reached down to pat the heads of the black beagle-labrador and the cocker spaniel. You had been allowed into their house, across the threshold. They were a family and you were a guest. Whenever their Dad entered the room, you were afraid to look at him directly, like the sun.

/

You had never seen anyone in your life who compelled you so entirely. He was always wearing fell running shoes that didn't match the rest of his outfit. He had close cut dark hair, a rich, enveloping voice and a kind laugh, days old stubble. His shirt was slightly open showing the hair on his chest, permanently tanned skin, sturdy shoulders under his blue suit. You remember his shoulders most of all because you wanted to touch them. Place your hands flat on them and look squarely into his hazel eyes. You wanted to be level with him. When he stood up, you realised you were exactly the same height.

/

First kiss on the bench in the garden, whisky-perfumed and warm. August. The kids away at their mum's house, just the two of you with a fire, the prurient stars above you and the wild lawn below and the dogs watching from the doorway. You were wearing his fleece jacket and it smelled of smoke and delicious sweat. Who leaned towards who? It felt like the movement of a seesaw. You didn't notice the cold. You were drunk on lemony moonlight and the silver outline of the eucalyptus tree, his nose against yours, the bristles on the back of his neck. You wanted to memorise every detail of his hands, chest, mouth. You talked about kids that first night, whether he wanted more. He did. He loved being a Dad. You were moving quickly and slowly, hurling yourself into the unknown, it was sudden and it had been happening forever. You recognised the pitch of him, the breath of him, the lean of him, the life of him, even as you were learning it.

/

Perhaps you crossed the threshold when you became a mother, carrying L. and B.'s half-brother. Your stomach felt doughy and promising in those days, though food made you sick, you hated smells that weren't sharp citrus. You made smoothies from blueberries and lemon peel and vanilla yoghurt. Your partner was at a conference. He texted to describe the fields outside Iowa City, the aching, ridiculous miles of them, the crops being fed by drone. You knew how they felt. Your body was an endless plot, persisting without you.

/

Notes for a sitcom. It is twilight, spring. Father and son are in the long queue for the auditorium together, clutching their separate tickets. They don't talk much. One of them has a hangover. Everyone in line is talking in hushed tones. They inch forwards. The father says the word pregnant. She's pregnant.

Because they booked late, because they got the cheap tickets, father and son are pulled in two different directions for their seats. Now they are in parallel lines, moving further apart. The son is mouthing *what the fuck*? They don't see each other again until after the performance. They go for a beer in the Brown Bear and talk about something else.

/

He tells B. in the car on the way back from her piano lesson. Later she will joke he was making sure she couldn't escape.

Outdoor cat

In those early days there was always
a ghost-cat, sitting on the ping pong table.
It sensed when it was being seen
and slinked off through nettles
under the low-hanging blackberry bush.

Grey coat, reverse omen – the memory
of a man who stopped mid-kiss
and said he loved you more
than his fiancée, did not
imagine he could live with you

so you came to feel you were
a lithe and feral thing, untreated,
calling at the kitchen door
but running if it came ajar
into backyard darkness,

known element, your body
invisible, those eyes
your only burden
only proof.

Passage

There is a gate
or perhaps an arched trellis
lavish with clematis,

a high coastal path
the coconut scent of gorse,
an overbearing sun

and the stones are rough,
you must watch
where you are going

watch yourself
from above
as you pass through

on bleached stones
carrying something
cool and oversized

desirable
because it is so
breakable.

Blanket

B's palm on your stomach
        once   moth-light
                in pregnancy

how she placed it there
        so tentatively
                your bodies

under one blanket
        TV burbling
                baby turning

in his private world
        her still hand
                a thousand ways

of never wanting
        to disturb.

On parenting

Sometimes, when the baby cried in his first months, B. would make sensible suggestions: *do you think he needs his dummy? Is his nappy dry?* She'd look tenderly down at him as if she was staring into water. She sang him tremulous songs. You said nothing. You did not trust yourself to get it right.

/

Your stepson can swing your son round his shoulders and swoop him down to the floor only to lift him high again at the last moment. He can wrestle him and box him and teach him to give high fives. He is just being himself. He has not been taught to fear dropping him. Your son squeals with giddy delight and you all get dizzy from watching.

/

Once, when your son was barely six months old and you were frayed at all your edges, his thin cry summoned you at 5.30 in the morning. Heavy footsteps on the stairs, a shadow by the nursery door. It was just L., coming home from a night out, arriving home as you were getting up. You said hello to him and he looked sheepish, muttered something about gap year life, then moved away, up the stairs to his attic room, still wearing his outdoor shoes.

You craved those nights-into-mornings, dancing in someone's kitchen with your friends passed out on the floor. But you were sailing into the long, sepia morning, three cups of coffee before 10 a.m., bouncy chairs and Teletubbies and endless tellings of *Fox's Socks. Poor old fox has lost his socks! Under the stair is a shirt to wear!*

When L. went out again that night, jacket slung over his shoulder, phone pinging with texts, part of you went with him into the city, just to remember what the air tasted like.

/

When you first thought about stepmothers and how you could write about them, you considered asking L. and B. to pen letters, describing what having step-parents feels like to them. You agonised about it for weeks. How could they be unfiltered if they thought you were going to read them? You decided the solution was to suggest a sealed envelope for the letters, one you could not open until some future point when and if they decided you could. But that is very little use in terms of understanding their reality at the point of writing. Also, you were afraid to ask. You worried that it would create a pressure, an expectation for them. Perhaps living in a blended family is about being wary, not sure whether you can ask, not certain that your needs will be granted, parent or child.

Fill a round glass with ice and pour a large gin into it. It has to be generous to taste the bitterness, not just the sweetness of tonic. Put your nose into the glass and inhale the peppery scent. Juniper berries. Mother's Ruin. Slice a crescent moon of lemon into the top and scatter in some frozen blackberries and redcurrants. In the bar earlier, a woman was telling a story about her stepmother. *My brother and I used to put her toothbrush down the toilet. We'd dip it in the bowl, then we'd put it back in the toothbrush holder so it was ready and waiting for her.* Laugh too loudly and too long. Take a gulp of your drink. *I'm sure you aren't that kind of stepmother* she added, touching you lightly on the arm.

The Juniper Tree

Germany. A wealthy couple pray every day for God to grant them a child.
In their courtyard is a huge evergreen, starred with blue berries. Juniper.

In winter, beneath its branches, the wife peels an apple. She cuts her finger
and drops of blood fall onto the snow. A month later, she gives birth

to a baby boy white as snow and red as blood. She dies of happiness.
The husband buries her under the juniper.

The new wife is not interested in trees. She loves morning sex and steak
cooked rare, glasses of Merlot soupy and warm as blood, the scent

of smoke on her clothes. She wears a strong perfume that some say
reminds them of garlic. They have a child, a daughter. The stepmother

only likes her stepson when he frowns and looks like his father.
When she decapitates the boy, there is surprisingly little mess

and the head rolls across the floor like a marble. So she gathers it up,
binds it to the rest of his body with a bandage and props his body

onto a chair outside, an apple resting on his lap. Later,
she's at the kitchen counter with a butcher's knife, turning him

into 'blood-soup'. When her husband comes home, they eat it
together. The bones are buried under the Juniper tree.

That night, under the ground, in the shelter of the tree, the bones
fuse together in the shape of a bird. There is a fine mist in the air

and the bird looks spectral as it burrows out of the ground, launches,
wings tipped purple and blue, chest the colour of a bruise.

Its eye is a juniper berry. It darts towards the town and as the sun rises,
it sings its life for all to hear

Once, you put on a pair of sensible, light flats and you landed in the centre of a woodland. Cloud trails in the sky above you, breadcrumb trails at your feet. You could sense movement on the edge of your vision, two children with a basket in the near distance and a slight woman departing in the other direction, walking quickly, glancing over her shoulder. Who to follow? Hansel and Gretel, their foray to the sickly house of the witch? Or the sly, persuasive stepmother who – out of need or fear – convinced her husband they couldn't afford to look after his kids? You don't want to know what the stepmother does when she thinks the children are disposed of. Maybe she reads a magazine and eats a sandwich. Maybe she starts repurposing their rooms. You watch her brisk shape vanishing. You are deep in the efficient darkness of the woods. A twig snaps. A bird reproaches you. You fall to your knees and you start to eat the breadcrumbs like a greedy animal, one by one.

On porn

Top Amazon results for search 'stepmother':

The Perfect Stepmother: A Totally Gripping Psychological Suspense Thriller
Evil Stepmothers: Season 1
My Stepmother is an Alien
The Young Step-mother OR A Chronicle of Mistakes
Stepmum starts down the path to Slutdom (free with Kindle Unlimited)
Saved from my Evil Stepmother by God
Stepmonster
Mommy Can Help: A collection of Taboo stories about Stepmothers and their Children (Available immediately, 18+)

Watch me, Alone

/

You've had boyfriends who insisted you watch stepmother porn with them. In one repeated scenario, a stepmother goes to look under her stepson's bed for magazines. She becomes inexplicably trapped there, her head and shoulders and arms under the bed. Cue the arrival of the stepson, who proceeds to strip her, push her bright pink lacy knickers to one side, expose her smooth, hairless cunt and fuck her coolly. The camera alternates between his thrusting buttocks and her open mouth and jiggling breasts. The idea here, you suppose, is to reverse the family power dynamic, sexualise a maternal figure, turn someone who might exercise authority over the son into someone he could bend over and penetrate.

In the porn industry, women in their twenties are often considered least lucrative as performers: they are said to fall into the gap between teen (the stepdaughter or student) and MILF (the horny stepmum). You imagine it as a yawning chasm, into which all the subtleties and ambiguities of the physical world, the body, drop one by one, whistling by as they fall.

They've been bound together with a thin length of twine. Unravelled, they fall leaf-soft to the floor. Danish slippers, mulberry red felt. Slip your hands into them first and wiggle your fingers around, enjoying their softness. Place one against your cheek. Slide your toes into them – how warm they feel inside. You aren't clutching the twine anymore, but gripping a sharp twig, a whip-sized length of tree. You're in a forest, everything seen through the gaps between trees. Autumn. Lazy sun dappling the surface of a lake. A splash, a gleeful shriek, a man's voice and a woman's. Tiptoe closer, keeping your body taut behind the slender trees. But now you are being pulled into the water, now you are in the bottom of the lake staring upwards at the woman's thighs, the skinny legs of the teenage boy. She is slightly tanned and he is pale. You see a mole, a scar, a stick-and-poke tattoo. A rushing, sucking sensation and now you're above them, looking down, sick with vertigo. Her hair is blonde, skimming her jaw. His is black, close-cropped. There is something clenched about his face. They're both laughing, abandoning themselves to the water, splashing and soaking one another. She screams as she plunges away and he dives after her.

On film

Here she is – the *Stepmom*. It's Julia Roberts playing Isabel, a young fashion photographer in a relationship with an older man – Luke – who already has a daughter and son from his marriage to his ex, Jackie. Isabel is allowed to be effortlessly glamorous – all oversized white shirts and large sunglasses – talented and hip, but never maternal. Each evening in her modernist dream house she slinks from room to room looking sexy, efficient, drinking chilled white wine and kissing Luke against tabletops. But by morning she's frazzled and incompetent, knowing nothing about what her impish stepson and grumpy teenage stepdaughter need, making them late for school, getting their packed lunches wrong, swearing and pouting and juggling work calls.

When Jackie, the mother, swoops in, she's generous and intuitive, baking for the kids and taking them horse riding. She's a former publisher turned stay-at-home mum, wounded by the divorce, criticising Isabel's parenting and career-ambitions. The role of Luke in all this is unclear. Mostly his function is to appear chiselled and long-suffering in his work shirt. He leaves the house early and returns late. He does showy parenting at the weekends, heroically steering rowing boats, making authoritative statements. He's happiest with everyone wanting him, occasionally irked by the pressures of being in demand. The women fight. He makes peace. That's the way it goes.

/

You watch another film and another. In the 1996 Philippine drama *Madrasta* (meaning stepmother), working-class Mariel marries wealthy Edward after his first wife abandons him – at the start of the film, we simply see the wife marching from the house, leaving a screaming baby behind her. With Edward at work, Mariel takes on responsibility as a mother to his three children. She's grudgingly accepted at times by the younger two, but the eldest daughter treats her with thinly disguised hostility. The household staff (for it is that kind of household) dislike her and insist on comparing her unfavourably to the ex. Mariel strives to win the acceptance and affection of her new stepchildren, through cooking, lavish presents and gestures which fall flat. Her anguish is almost unwatchable, a mounting sense of despair and abandonment. There is something uncanny about the whole film, as if she is sleepwalking through a house which wants to eject her.

In *Stepmom*, Susan Sarandon and Julia Roberts are granted their reconciliation eventually, their truce, but the plot device feels like an abdication. The ultimate cop out: Jackie is revealed to be suffering from terminal cancer and everyone flocks to her side. One night, Jackie invites Isabel to have dinner with her, and they bond when Isabel reveals her admiration for Jackie's maternal instincts, while Jackie praises Isabel's 'coolness' as a means to connect with her teenage daughter Anna. Isabel finally lets her guard down when she tells Jackie her biggest fear is that on Anna's wedding day, all she will wish for is her mother's presence, while Jackie admits her own fear is that she will be forgotten. On Christmas morning, the family celebrate together. Jackie is nearing the end of her life and calls the children to her bedside one by one. Isabel takes a family portrait of Luke and Jackie with the children. In a poignant gesture, Jackie beckons Isabel over, 'Let's get a photo with the whole family.' As the credits roll, the women are shown side by side, holding hands. Jackie will always have their past and Isabel will have their future.

Why do you find this ending so unsatisfactory? In a certain light it is touching, inspiring even. Women, supporting each other. A true blended family. But it troubles you. No, it angers you. Two women set in structural competition: the only way to make a truce is to kill off one of them. Bitch or martyr. Which would you rather?

/

You think of a documentary you saw about Rio Ferdinand and his partner Kate – they married after the death of his first wife Rebecca. Kate became a stepmum to the three young children, and the show focused on her struggle to adapt. What struck you most was how she couldn't dislike the mother, perfected as she was by death. Any difficult emotion was doubly tinged: when Kate felt uncomfortable about Rio and Rebecca's wedding photos being on display in the house, she also felt monstrous for objecting.

/

One of the most moving things you ever read was a letter in the *Guardian* from a biological mother to a stepmother, thanking her for the job she'd done with her daughter:

'You navigated the difficult teenage years with calm resilience. You kept boundaries in place even when she pushed them. You knew consistency was important, and you'd call me to check on curfews and ground rules.'

Such dialogues make you weep. You cannot imagine being that kind of admired woman, steering an effective course.

'She didn't need another mother; you knew that, and you shaped your own role in her life. For that, I will always be grateful.'

There are special mothers' day cards for stepmoms, inclusive gifts, tailored journals and cakes and all the accoutrements of capitalism. You have never received one, but it is comforting to know they exist.

/

Why is Rio Ferdinand's partner so loveable? Why does she always make the children's sandwiches? Why has she always managed to style her hair so it falls like silk over her shoulder? Why doesn't she go into the front garden at night and fall to her knees and try to fit the whole moon in her mouth? Why doesn't she tear all the beautiful photos down off the wall? Why doesn't she rage more? Why doesn't she rage?

Felt

The time you took B. to a felting workshop to make tiny ornamental dogs
& you worked side-by-side, learning the knack of it, shapelessness needled
into elegance – if you prod at something long enough your fingers
bloom new blood
but in the end a body forms as bodies will
& in small ways (a nose, an outstretched paw) it starts to bear
resemblance to a life.

On perspective

You seem unhealthily preoccupied with the term you. Yes you. Who else do you think it could refer to? *You* is a reminder of being accosted by strangers, by teachers across the playground: *hey you. Yes, I'm talking to you.* Therefore you are trying to accost yourself.

/

Your friend P. tells you that her youngest stepdaughter borrowed her shirt: cream, with tiny, dark buttons on it. All week the stepdaughter denied it. Then P. was browsing her Instagram page and there it was, proud as milk. Her stepdaughter had tied it round herself in a fetching way and she was pouting into the camera with dark berry lipstick on and her hair freshly straightened. Later that night the shirt appeared on P.'s bed, as if it had never been anywhere. It smelled of strange perfume. She held it up to her face and inhaled.

/

Lines written on the way back from dropping your stepdaughter at school in the dead of winter with no coat on. Lines written on holiday during the joint pedicure, the family game of badminton. Lines written when you were all crammed into a hotel room together, pretending to sleep. Lines spoken aloud when she had her noise cancelling headphones on. Lines written while failing to make crispy tofu with garlic and salt. Lines formed by the wet towels on bedroom floors. Lines written between good luck messages and happy birthday texts. Lines written in lipstick she borrowed from your make up drawer. Lines written when you were trying, trying not to be jealous of her figure. Lines written in the ink of her first handpicked tattoo and the ink of your latest design, your pictures that keep on multiplying because the less you know yourself, the more you need. Lines written to the sound of the washing machine, by the light from the midnight fridge. Lines made in her cigarette ash in your favourite bowl. Drunk lines. Heartfelt lines. Lines written face down on the bed. Lines written when you were both in the same house, quietly coexisting.

/

B. tries on your favourite pair of trousers, burnt orange and darted at the waist, rusty and comfortable. She gives a twirl. Before you can stop yourself, you're telling her to keep them. After all, they look so much better on her.

/

So often you look at B. and feel a pride you have no right to. Her eclectic music taste, knowledge of the '80s, her easy generosity with strangers. Her voice – spun sugar and glass. Her appreciation of film and her acute sense of injustice. The instinct she feels to wrap dogs in blankets and tuck them in. Lime-sharp curiosity. Her resolute refusal to accept help. In the house, you walk around the same space in your own worlds, the rooms rattling with your footsteps. Cups of shared tea. The scent of frying eggs. Hand gestures, semaphore of care.

Summer

You see her through the roadside window
of the corner bar, gorgeous as a stranger,
in mom jeans and a waistcoat you once gave to her.

She's carrying a tray of cocktails.
The central glass is fluted, amber bubbles
sparking under strips of light. She must not spill

this suddenly electric gift. You stand
on the pavement, braced. A greyhound passes
with its shadow still intact

and as she turns her back, you find
you have your right hand lifted in a sort of wave.
The moment is years, is rush hour traffic

streaming home, a blue tinge,
that thing hanging over you – the sky,
you mean, you guess.

ii.

You entered the silence when you entered the room.
Or you entered the silence because there was no room,

or you wrote enter the silence and the silence
made it so. Enter silence with the character of snow –

long-predicted, temporary, turning to barely-there
a fire escape that leads you out into thin air, feet

still treading nothing. Silence as an end in itself,
or silence exiting, pursued by nothing but itself.

You entered the silence before and the silence after
and the silence left by the ever-after. Or we entered

the silence and we ruined it forever, we filled it
with us – we were a front, impending weather

in its clear sky. We passed silence between us
like a kiss, and somewhere in the process

missed the point: silence entered can't be shared
unless it's silence falling everywhere, silence as condition,

as future tense, silence as treatment for offence,
or silence as a tall fence between where we are

and where we thought we'd be. Or none of this. Or I
was just the silence and you entered me.

You are speaking out of turn, though you don't know what it would mean to speak 'in turn', you have lost track of when your turn is: you are neither the head of your household nor a dependent, not an authority figure but a woman responsible for cleaning the toilets and freshening the towels and providing dinner on time and making sure the fridge is stocked with the right kind of milk. You are not allowed to have opinions about matters of The Stepchildren but you must make sure you are not being selfish in relation to them. All this makes you want to be profoundly selfish. You start with minor acts of rebellion, buying new clothes for yourself when you know you can't afford to. Putting your best toiletries in a drawer where they cannot be easily found. Hiding your hairdryer. Inventing reasons to be out of the house, errands and work, then hiding away in a cafe and writing for an hour in your new jacket, hitting the keys hard as if you are doing something very important. Pouring a glass of white wine while you're cooking the dinner and looking cross when anyone else enters the kitchen.

Stepmother

It helps to think you are
        a pink pomelo t-shirt, someone's summer best

and you've been draped across
        the lovely sheets, neat socks and plain white tees

so now you're balled up
        with the dirty laundry of the house

conspicuous, so frivolously bright –
        cocktail umbrella, quartered cherry in a tin of fruit –

and in the quiet violence of the wash
        you can't help leaking into everything.

Then, when the drum's unloaded
        it's all muted salmon, tidemarked,

something like the aftermath
        of blood and – yes – there's beauty

in the novelty of this new shade,
        a kind of softening, but since your touch

will anything come clean?
        Will anything be worn outside again?

Yes, you invent your own Fairy Godmother. You need someone to see you as you are, make you a pumpkin carriage, send you to the ball (you SHALL go to the ball), take your apron off and dress you in satin. Your fairy godmother will be a woman from Belfast with a broken nose. Your fairy godmother will listen to punk music and buy you pizza. Your fairy godmother will own many disguises, you'll never know where your godmother will appear next! There: smoking a joint in the alcove outside Sainsbury's, offering you a drag. There: walking with such authority, so slowly across the road the drivers don't mind waiting. There; savouring the bitterness of a double espresso, in a high stool by the window of the one authentic Italian cafe in town. Your godmother has impeccable taste. Your godmother will know when you are in pain, when you're checking yourself for punctures, patting up and down your own body, trying to work out where the fault lies.

Brain

You're awake when you should be asleep
and asleep when you should be awake.

For all our sakes, I wish you'd pack it in,
pack up, take all your shit with you,

and join the circus of somebody else's head
or build a little violent house of thoughts

from your base materials – false hope
and dread. I've tried to wear you out

with exercise: no-pull harness, extender leash
but you're all collar-slip and quick release,

you're a bored kid in the supermarket
reaching to grab pink party biscuits from the shelf

and there's my heart trundling across, predictable.
She's a knackered parent and despite herself

she loves you, knowing you're the only one
she's got. I raise my fingers to my temple

miming *are we giving this a shot?*

Sertraline

I like to think I'm special to you, although
I know you have so many special friends
here, in the dark heart of the year

when even the neighbour's rowan
scrapes against the window, plaintive,
with that sound everyone hated as a child.

What days I have seem shorter than ever
and all my jackets are unsuitable for any
weather. Far safer undercover, hoarding

lamplight, paper, the memory of lavender,
as the tiny seed of you rolls in my palm
or catches in the throat, ignites a radiance.

Still, you make me sick. I love you fiercely
in secret, like all the others
too old now to be called girls.

I wish you didn't give them what you give
to me, wish you weren't given
so freely. Last night in the dispensary,

I watched a woman shake her red hair
loose – she made the queue seem elegant,
passing with her paper bag, her smile

that let me know you're also hers,
that once, at least, you made her feel
good too. Go on. Admit it. Didn't you?

On betrayal

In every fairytale, the promise of a broken word.

Swear you will go to –

Swear you will never touch –

The woods behind the castle. The river with its small, unstable bridge.
The places where the smashed words are hoarded.

The problem with Fairy Godmothers is that you can't control when they appear. The staged entrance, the grand flourish: this is their modus operandi. They have the prerogative to leave before answering questions.

Fairy Godmother

Since no one's turning
kitchen mice
to stallions for you,

nobody will pimp
that Braeburn up
into a stately chariot,

you'll have to start
from scratch. Stand
by the field boundary

at sunset in your worst
dressing gown, a fine rain
muddling your hair,

practise appearing
to yourself. Accept your
chill hands, the prying wind.

Once you're convinced
you're here, climb
the barbed fence,

walk through crop stubble
to a minor vantage point
from which you might

rehearse the art of luminosity:
this means unthinking
everything

you've taken in
since being a child. Return
the trees to dancing skeletons.

Look the hedgerow
into wire wool.
Your bare feet in the mud

are living things, rabbits
perhaps, moving soft,
without your bidding.

Once unlocked, the trick,
works anywhere. The sky
is vellum or fresh cream.

Winter: your friend
arriving in a grey cape
with porridge, blackout curtains

for the house. There will be
men your gaze cannot redeem,
nor can you do the Jesus trick

of Evian to Chardonnay.
But look – the house sparrows
become fleet messengers,

diagonals of sun on bark
are all the fire you need
and even your own body

can be abundant; not a prison,
just a cage with hinged doors –
you open your mouth

and all the quick things
of the world escape
from you, silvery, with tiny

beating hearts to make
their own way, make their home
in the air.

On mothering

The stepmother, of course, simply does not exist without the idea of the mother. What is your idea of mother? Most of your first recollections involve your gran and her house next door, chalk on the driveway, pretending to ride a bike into a forgotten realm. Your mother exists in them as an absence, not necessarily because she was absent, but because mothers are hard to look directly at, like the sun.

You remember going through her wardrobe while she cooked downstairs. The faint mothy smells of the skirts, fabrics you ignored because they would swamp you. It was the shoes you were interested in, the ones with heels, her cream patent sling backs. You could slip your small feet into them and stand upright, tall, pretending to be glamorous. You made sure to put them back exactly as they had been.

/

What was it like for your mother to grow up with a stepmum? All your memories of your grandad's partner Clare are of calling her Auntie, of scampi and chips for tea and Brummie vowels and pretending to be a mermaid in the bath, eating marshmallows in bed at midnight, watching musicals with her and your grandad and singing along too loudly. You didn't understand how she was different from your grandma or why your mum was sometimes less irritable with her than she was with her own mother. Clare made sandwiches with the crusts cut off for Sunday teatime and had a sour faced Siamese cat. She loved to feed the ducks in Sutton Park with you. When your grandad went blind in his retirement, your mum and Clare would go away together on gardening trips. For years you imagined them kneeling together, enjoying the intimacy of soil, worms and twigs through their fingers. But when you saw the photographs, they were walking round the gardens of stately homes, resplendent in August sun. Once your mum told you that they visited a grounds where there were so many frogs it was impossible to walk across the lawn without stepping on their tiny bodies and crushing them underfoot. Clare couldn't bear it, she said, she would never hurt a fly.

/

After your grandad died you went to stay overnight with Clare before the funeral. You took a small black whippet with you, a stray you'd adopted in Cumbria. You walked for miles in the snow with her. Clare swaddled it in blankets and cushions at bedtime. 'I don't think your mum will mind,' she said. 'She's such a sweet creature'. It wasn't clear who she meant.

The next day, the dog pissed nervously on the landing and your mum accused you of ruining the whole day.

/

When Clare started forgetting things, your mum spent more and more time in Sutton Coldfield, getting her shopping, writing every appointment and milestone in the calendar, repeating things in a loud voice. When Clare put the plug-in kettle on the hob and set fire to it, she started to think about a diagnosis. But there was another blood relative who didn't like the idea. *They're trying to say you're potty, Clare. She isn't even your real daughter is she?*

/

Clare's eyes became watery and distant. You took her on holiday to Berwick-upon-Tweed and every night she was bemused by your son, asked who he belonged to. She called him The Baby. Festooned in white blankets, frail as a bird, she had begun to look like a baby herself. She walked the corridors at night and came into your room by mistake. She enjoyed strawberry ice cream, eaten with a tiny spoon, so cold it made her shudder. She liked the wind on the beach, blown straight from Scotland. She giggled when your son taught himself to crawl, thumping his hands and knees across the wooden floor.

When Clare went into hospital for the last time and visitors weren't allowed, your mum sent anguished messages every day. Letters to Loved Ones, the service was called. Clare died in the morning but she wasn't told. Mum was still sending letters at lunchtime, posting them into silence.

/

What you remember is this: your mum standing in the driveway at Sutton Coldfield and mouthing through the glass at Clare with tears streaming down her face. She was saying I love you, making the gestures big like a pantomime. You never knew if Clare could really hear her.

/

Imagine a small girl – maybe ten, maybe eleven – walking home from school. Imagine she looks like your mother. Imagine she sees a woman who looks like your grandmother at a bus stop, kissing a stranger. The view, a kaleidoscope, a lens turned into focus. She makes herself get home, put her key in the door. When the mother returns, the girl doesn't know how to ask about what she saw, so instead she puts her book down and wonders out loud: *do you still love me?*

Isn't that the only question? We ask it for centuries, carefully, without moving our lips.

Two women

<table><tr><td>Beryl is married
to Norman</td><td>Clare is married
to Alf.</td></tr></table>

Their work is the ache of the factory

In Birmingham, bomb damage is never far off.
The city of their birth has missing ribs.

<table><tr><td>Beryl dances
for her life</td><td>Clare is the best
dancer</td></tr></table>

Their men steal flowers for them from
other people's gardens.

A-line skirts. Martini and lemonade.

<table><tr><td>Beryl is
pregnant</td><td>Clare is
with Alf</td></tr></table>

Kingstanding. Perry Barr and Perry Park.
Streets of their hard-won houses.

<table><tr><td>Beryl has lung damage
a daughter</td><td>Clare has
no daughter</td></tr></table>

They cheer the men at football in the cold.
Sometimes, there are holidays.

When does a life start to evacuate?

now Beryl is   Clare is
with Alf   without

Off cuts at the butchers on Fridays.
A silence lasting longer than it should.

The shadow of a man's shirt
as it hangs on the washing line.

Now Beryl   now Clare
is with Alf   is with Norman.

Between them, they have a daughter.
        Listen – she's waking up.

Gra

The story of the old woman and the undying sun
makes me think of you, Gra, in your school uniform,

crawling through a concrete pipe on the building site
that was your playground, emerging dirty

and unscathed – unlikely, wished for, like
the dawn itself, taken-for-granted light.

You, throwing bricks through the Salvation Army window
and escaping blame, the smashed glass

the jagged cartoon sun in picture books.
You, finding the body of your father in the kitchen,

slumped, inanimate, your father who had been so cruel
but who would always rise each morning,

cough, go out to paint and decorate the world. At sixteen,
you knew the sun was not undying,

but you went along with it, the story of your life, a sequence,
the empty rooms your older brother chased you through

with a pickaxe handle, the door split wide
all over a tiny wheel of cheese and how he held it afterwards

aloft, framed by the window and the blue sky behind,
a golden, cul-de-sac eternity.

Matabryne

And when her son's wife produced seven children
- seven! - in one dreary afternoon
each with a silver chain around their neck,

the grandmother knew that they were too much world
and swore she'd kill them. So she turned them into puppies
but they rolled into a writhing ball and squirmed from her

and she plunged after them, thinking of drowning,
flames and banishment, but every time
they rose from nothing, slow as lifting mist.

They turned to swans and flew and one became feather
itself, became a dart of fire, so he could cleave to her
and turn her into last rites, her own pyre.

TB

When I try to write the word, I'm stopped short
by a splintering, some violence

like a ribcage cracking, or being cracked from outside,
which is different, which is worse.

How can you describe a pain impossible
in your own lifetime? Abstract

as someone else's love song, love scene.
Etc. Each night I have to dream

your death, without
knowing how it feels.

When I burned my fingers as a child or
had a splinter needled out and cried

you'd say, *I hope that's the worst pain*
you ever have to know

and it seemed so scornful, but you meant it
sincerely, you meant *I spare you*

I give you permission
to be spared.

Red

In the woods, in the bed of a house
the wolf has long-since taken over

Grandma waits inside his body
as the acids do their slowest work on her

and where she was once thought kindly,
stooped and hooded, now she's fierce

with what was always in her heart,
a viscous anger rising, frothing

coming out now through the gaps
in his butter-coloured teeth.

Weight

It seems made-up:
that I can carry my grandmother

from the lintel of the doorway
to the waiting car

her weight reduced to
something less than child,

the paper figures
we'd cut out when I was small

row after row of them
pliant witnesses

unfolded
still holding hands

Seek

My son is searching for my grandmother
in the last blue bed she lay in.

He runs to find her. He is so theatrical,
waiting to be proved right. And when her body is

not there, he's undefeated, quizzical.
He calls her name three times,

she must be in the sun, in the conservatory
because she liked it there

so he pads across that room
of striped shadows, window flung open

to air the house. The breeze
ruffles the hair of the spider plant.

Alfie, look closer, she's hiding
in your long-limbed shadow,

framed at the threshold, she's in
the ice-melt centre of your mother's eyes.

The shoes wail at you. Why have you abandoned them? You shrug. Your feet are bare and blistered these days. You have forgotten how to walk. Better to crawl on your belly along the ground, to become properly acquainted with it.

Serpent – from the French 'to creep'. You try to make your presence on the stairs unfelt. You are quiet when you should speak. What are you doing in this house if not creeping?

On snakeskin

A tiny museum near Oldham, a place of curiosities. There were stuffed owls and retrieved stones and feathers. But all you really remember is the largest tank, something pale and coiled and papery, completely motionless. Close up, it had to be a dead thing. You only breathed again when you saw the snake, away in the corner, utterly intact. Coil as trace, an old skin. Texture of history, self-ghost. If only you could work so efficiently.

/

In the bath one teatime, your son insists you have to play at being snakes. Two snakes.

I am the boy snake and you are the Mummy snake, he says. *Together we will fight!*

He is sitting at the opposite end of the bath to you, his curved tummy poking out of the water, his pursed lips and his serious expression and the musty, buttery scent of his unwashed hair making him unmistakably yours. He holds your ankles, then he manoeuvres himself so he can slither on his stomach up along your legs. You are both slippery from the water, silky almost.

Hisssssss, he says, *hisssss*

He stops when he's lying flat on your torso. Then he flings his arms around your neck and announces *I love you Mummy snake* and presses his cheek against yours. You could hold him like this forever, so close, like when he was born and bloody.

Now, he says, *you be the boy snake and I'm the Mummy snake. I know how to be a Mummy snake*, he adds. *It's easy.*

/

In the mornings now, it's your habit to check yourself for signs of serpentry. You feel elongated. To accommodate their narrow bodies, snakes' paired organs (such as kidneys) do not appear side by side, but one in front of another, a sort of dignified queue inside the body. Most only have one functional lung. Your breath barely steams the mirror. A new lack. You know that the world's largest snake is the reticulated python, up to seven metres long, but you can't imagine its scale. The word 'reticulated' puts you in mind of articulated lorries.

You stick your tongue out and probe the air, imagining what it would be like to know everything that way, to collect particles and draw them in for analysis, to taste the complicated air. You think of how much a first taste tells you – the intensity never matched by the next bite – or how much you can know about someone from the way they kiss. The knowledge of the body that the mind revises, over-confident editor, certain of its rights.

/

You have always seen Medusa as the ultimate victim, the ultimate doomed sex symbol. When you think about the women in your life, when you conjure them from nothing, at night, in silence, each of them is looking back over one shoulder, fixing the level of a deliberate stare. That's your image of Medusa: her unmoving expression and her writhing hair. As if she is the stone, not who she gazes on. She seems fixed in time, stilled by the injustice of her rape by Poseidon, her betrayal by Athena. Her eyes are clouding violet: perhaps she is thinking of renouncing her old layer of skin, slithering out untethered and buffed. Even like this, nobody can look away from her.

/

The female of the species is more deadly than the male. Rudyard Kipling said it first, but you always imagine Space singing those lyrics, all floppy fringes and slim hips. You used to revel in that, in the promiscuity of birds, the dangerous power of female spiders who just as often eat their suitors as mate with them. You'd think of the male black widow, who must guess whether the female is hungry from the sex pheromones in her silk, the orb weaver who waits patiently at the edge of the web, the nursery web spider who sneaks into the female's web and binds her with his silk threads so he can mate with her.

You feel a thrill at these accounts of power, because you don't know your own. Perhaps you are Lady Tremaine, Snow White's ageing enemy, transfixed by the stepmother in the mirror. Perhaps the way you have begun to think of other women's bodies – softness and angles equally enthralling – is a sign of ultimate narcissism.

/

What are you doing here, in this text, day after day but assembling scales, trying to make a skin to live in?

There have been so many resentments. The girls who laughed at you at school and called you boyish after you lost so much weight your bones showed. Your boyfriend's best female friend at University, so tall she seemed to be a supermodel, the one he looked at with thinly-disguised longing, the one who had better taste in music than you, more money, more class, longer, thicker hair. All the other women you've been set against, compared unfavourably to, women you've wronged and slandered. Famous women, gilded by Photoshop. Authority figures, mother substitutes. What good was in any of it? Where did it lead you? Here. Only here.

Bitterns

Heard but not seen, our desire grows
in the reed beds – *bitter,*

bitterest – for what it cannot have
under a limestone-coloured sky.

We almost missed the marsh-harrier
the nesting short-eared owl.

We listened to the man who cried out
bittern at a startled pheasant.

In the hide, I tried to look before
you had opened the window.

The herons were patient and lugubrious.
A single branch was moving

like a wiper, back and forth
across the wetlands' misty screen

and once seen, I could not
unsee that, my want was driving

roughshod over reclaimed coalfields
tentative nests, eggs held secret

in their twine. I had something
in my throat, a longing

pebble-shaped and cold
enough to choke on

and I coughed it up
perhaps with the thought

of offering it to you, to see
what you might make of it, quietly

there, down in the silt, glimpsed
through the strips of reeds.

Weathervane

My son can't sleep. He's worried about reincarnation:
What happens Mum, if I come back an owl and you're a mouse?
I tell him they wouldn't do that, though I don't believe it.
Slowly, he uncurls into sleep while I sit beside the bed
thinking how, in life-after-life, I'd come back as a glacier mouse,
a small moss-covered stone, or a wind-directed flag
outside the museum in Qeqertarsuaq, anything moved
by something greater than its mass. A blade of grass that bends.
A varved section of ice, or water scooped from metres deep
below a frozen lake and poured into a large container to be
analysed valued no matter what it showed. Or any of the
quirks of ice ice apron, ice cauldron or ice blade, ice gruel, ice
limit, ice-scour lake, ice lens, the place where layers change
or I'd be snowblink, iceblink, snowpillar and snowglide
something slender, spinning on a church roof,
bound by the myth of prediction. My son, we only get
one life and we let it buffet us. I'd trust myself to sycamore,
to land wherever you are.

That night you go back to the cupboard, tipsy. Inside the darkness, the box is empty. The shoes are all gone. It is as if you have been robbed. You scan for evidence, signs of disarray, things being upended, but it is neat and orderly, this new absence. All is tidy, the way you said you always wanted things.

On stepfathers

The children, your stepchildren, of course, have a stepfather, their mum's new husband. When you first found the shoes, when you first started to write this down compulsively, you thought about emailing him and asking how he copes, if he ever feels inadequate, if he feels pushed to the sidelines of his own life.

But there is no wicked stepfather writ large. There are no fairytales about men who join blended families and become poisoned by jealousy, who find their stepsons a threat to their own vanity, who treat the children with thinly-veiled hostility, who send them to the centre of a dense woodland and leave them there, trapped by briars, to lie down with the rotted summer and crushed tin cans and extinguished teenage campfires.

/

There are men who are praised for 'taking on' another man's family, like Conrad Anker in the film about American climber Alex Lowe, sitting in the remnants of his best friend's life, describing for the camera how he wanted to look after the three boys after their father was buried in a skiing accident on Shishapangma, how his friendship with their mother ionised into love. Conrad, in his plaid blue shirt, sandy hair swept over his crown, facing any hostility with solid, willed indifference, shedding tears, standing on the sidelines, in the kitchen, waiting for the boys to recognise him. He is martyred by his love, his respect for his lost friend, his loyalty to the family he left behind. All that tumult, encased in snow, preserved in ice, like the body of George Mallory Anker discovered on Everest in 1999, just before his ill-fated trip with Alex.

There are a thousand kinds of stepfather. There are angry ones, violent ones, ones who repeat the mistakes of the father. There are downtrodden overlooked ones, bored ones, ecstatic ones. But all of them are allowed to be singular. There is no handed-down story, no Disney villain, no grand representative of the type.

You could ask the children's stepfather how he feels about this, but you don't because –

/

The woman you call The Ex is a stepmother to her new husband's children. It is her you should speak to, her you should interview and confide in, but you cannot bring yourself to. You cannot be vulnerable in front of each other. You tried once when you were pregnant and your words hung in the air like sad, ragged birthday bunting, left up because nobody could be bothered to take it down.

Sometimes your son insists that The Ex lives at your house, that she lives with you all. You tell him that he's wrong, she has her own house, but he becomes indignant. And then you think, perhaps he's right after all.

/

B.'s 16th birthday party. Summer. The Ex's house. Everyone is polite. You get mildly drunk and go to the playground. She walks the dog and you walk with your son, holding hands. The others are trailing behind. You admire the scarf she is wearing, her jumpsuit, her haircut. You talk about work and about the difficulties of shaping thoughts into books. Your son chatters away. She is familiar to him. She's been kind to him since he was born, gifting him a soft, velvety grey and white panda, just like the ones the older children had when they were small. Is she family to him? In a way, yes. And why shouldn't she be? If you are allowed to love her children, why shouldn't she be allowed to love yours? You find yourself wondering if you could have been friends, real friends, if you met in different circumstances, if there was no complicated sense of old passions, possession and sex and power. Maybe it's her you're obsessed with. You're a moth, orbiting a flame.

The next day, B. comes down the stairs in flared jeans and you notice she is wearing your soft leather Doc Martens. You recognise each scuff on the toes. You have the same shoe size now, she's getting taller every day and maybe soon she'll be taller than you. She's already taller than her mother. She smiles shyly and you smile back and she picks up her flask of coffee and goes out into the winter morning, overnight frost jewelled on the windscreens of cars, the pavements slippery, a kingdom of new ice. You watch her departing feet, you pay them great attention. She is going to the bus stop, then on through the rush hour to college where she'll learn how to frame the perfect photograph, how to assemble a scene. All day your shoes will carry her, the way you've broken and worn them changing her walk subtly, your strange imprint out of place in a world of teenage canteens and park cider and street protests, the kind you never had the nerve for.

On jealousy

You have wasted so much time in your life fearing other women. When you were pregnant, you felt dizzy with relief when you knew you weren't having a girl – this is an admission to be whispered, it is shameful, vindictive even. There have been places and times where baby girls are murdered for their gender and by having that brief thought it's as if you have aligned yourself with them, as if you have a secret violence in you. It was only born of dread: you were afraid that you'd be more likely to pass on your own self-loathing, your wrenching insecurities. You remember being eleven years old and plump and happy in your cycling shorts, your own mother passing you in the living room and stopping to comment on the size of your bottom, how ludicrous it was at your age. Your mother insists this didn't happen, so you can't explain how you think the shorts were purple and that you were standing next to the kitchen doorway, half in shadow and half in sunlight, cleaved neatly in two.

/

Your partner's mother has mistakenly called you by The Ex's name. His sister too. When you were sleepless with your son, both of you blundering through the foggy days, he'd say her name when he meant yours. He's even called your son by her surname, as if he was hers. At a party in Sussex, an old friend introduced you to someone else as her. You felt detached from yourself then, as if you really were sleepwalking through someone else's life, miming their gestures, a passable imitation of the real thing. And you would curse her in your mind, as if she were the one speaking.

/

Jealousy of his nicknames for her, the way they divided their furniture so that all the lamps in your house once belonged to her, the way they influenced each other's taste. And yes, admit it, jealousy of their beautiful children, the fact that they made them together, the bond between them that can never – must never – break.

/

What a waste. So many women angry with each other, for the space they occupy in men's lives. And the stepmother as the poster-child for this: she occupies, she comes into the nest and squats there, grim-feathered. No wonder she is a threat, an obscure danger. But she in turn is brutalised by the space she sits in, the still-warm imprint of the other, the aftermath of the 'true' mother, the one who was always there first, no matter what, no matter how 'good' she manages to be. This is why she becomes a serpent: so she can coil herself small, so she can slither through the gaps.

/

The shoes are not there the next night, or the next. Now, you only go back to compulsively check on their absence. There was a grand beginning to this, a big reveal, but there is no conclusive ending. What you see in the empty box is up to you.

Miles and miles of women, wearing each others' shoes, walking in them to see how they pinch or swamp, how they feel, how tall they make you feel. Women swapping with each other, helping each other finish off an outfit. Not because the foot is interchangeable, but because they can share what they have. And then one day they will recognise the shoes for what they are, an adornment, a taught fashion, a trope.

Take your shoes off. Take your shoes off and throw them in the lake. Take your shoes off and bury them by the cat's ashes at the foot of the rowan tree. Take them off and hide them in the chimney. Stow them in the dampest corner of the cellar. Send them to the moon and stars. Take off your shoes and put them in a story, make them into a vase, a coaster, a parable, a song. But take them off, take them off, even if just for a moment, take it all off.

On stories

In this, the fairytale stepmother you are building can stand tall, hold her head high. If she is a snake, she can slip fluidly through her stepchildren's lives, adapt to their shape. She can be unobtrusive, living in the pauses between things, and this makes her a better witness.

You will never remind them of themselves, that shudder of dawning recognition. You will never remind them of their mother, swim towards them like a reflection. You can look at them dispassionately and like them, admire them, with full knowledge of their flaws. There is no sense of predisposition. It will change over time, the way you dance around each other. There are no givens and that makes for adventure.

You did not pick your stepchildren. Nor did they pick you. But every day you can choose to love each other, without the biases of biology, the contractual obligations of a blood-tie. They see the worst of you and you see the worst of them. And you stay. And they speak to you. And they trust you with their fears and irritations and joys. They eat the food you make. You trade Christmas gifts and worry about what each other will think. It is, in its way, an opportunity. You cannot trade on unconditional love, but you can create the conditions of love. You can refuse to give up on each other.

If the shoe no longer fits –

If you ever go to the Ex's
door, alone, to ask for her
forgiveness, you will go
shoeless and you will say –

Acknowledgements

The greatest thanks go to Sarah Howe, superlative editor. You have shaped this manuscript into what it is.

Thank you to Arts Council England for a DYCP grant which enabled early formal experiments with this book. Thanks too to Sheffield libraries for allowing me to host a workshop on stepmother fairytales, generously giving me space.

Thank you to Fleur Shorthouse for helping me navigate stepmother stories.

I owe a debt of gratitude to the many stepmothers who contributed anonymously to research I carried out in 2021 – 2022 asking about experiences of entering and forging blended families. All of the things you shared – so candidly, so generously – informed and altered the text. These poems are for all of you, but especially Barbara Crossley who sadly died before the completion of the manuscript. Barbara, thank you for all our conversations about the figure of the stepmother and much more besides. You are greatly missed.

Thank you to Rachel Bower, Alan Buckley, Declan Ryan, Suzannah Evans for early readings and feedback on individual poems.

Thanks above all to my birth family, blended family, chosen families.

About the Author

Helen Mort has published three collections of poetry: *Division Street* (2013), *No Map Could Show Them* (2016) and *The Illustrated Woman* (2022) and has been shortlisted for the Forward, T. S. Eliot and Costa prizes. She is also the author of a novel, *Black Car Burning* (2019) and creative non-fiction including *A Line Above the Sky* (2022) and *Ethel* (2024). She is a professor at Manchester Metropolitan University and lives in Sheffield.